Poems
of the
Day

Praise for *Poems of the Day: The Ramblewood*

"This slim volume of 31 personal observations (mostly about ordinary domestic issues like marriage and motherhood) brings with it a welcome dose of skill and panache that makes it more than meditation. Walker's writing is sometimes lyrical, sometimes surprising (as when she has to remind herself that she loves the baby, and no, she's not really going to throw him out the window), sometimes simply the passionate love letter to her family at its core."

—Ellyn Bache, award-winning author of
nine novels including *Safe Passage* and winner
of the Willa Cather Fiction Prize

"Inspirations about Love and Mothering, Divine and Otherwise. A word bath of imagery evoking worshipful submersion in Nature, simple and profound. To the question, 'Where do we come from?' she answers, 'I wish you waves crashing out loud the sound of Peace.' A worthy collection."

—Beth Larson Sherk, teacher, playwright, and
novelist; author of *The River's Bend*

Poems of the Day

THE RAMBLEWOOD

Courtney Jett Walker

Belle Isle Books
www.belleislebooks.com

Copyright © 2024 by Courtney Jett Walker

No part of this book may be reproduced in any form or by any electronic or mechanical means, or the facilitation thereof, including information storage and retrieval systems, without permission in writing from the publisher, except in the case of brief quotations published in articles and reviews. Any educational institution wishing to photocopy part or all of the work for classroom use, or individual researchers who would like to obtain permission to reprint the work for educational purposes, should contact the publisher.

ISBN: 978-1-962416-39-9
Library of Congress Control Number: 2024914257

Designed by Sami Langston
Project managed by Hannah Tonsor

Printed in the United States of America

Published by
Belle Isle Books (an imprint of Brandylane Publishers, Inc.)
5 S. 1st Street
Richmond, Virginia 23219

belleislebooks.com | brandylanepublishers.com

To Jamie, Ella, Ranen, Shelby, and Holden.

Thank you my darling, my dear! I love you to the moon and back again! You are my sunshine! It's so nice to have you back where you belong! Over the rainbow, under the sea, and all the way back to meeeeeee!

Contents

Preface xi
Day One: The Ramblewood 1
Day Two: Fade Up the Skylights 3
Day Three: What You Dream Your Life to Be 4
Day Four: What Is True 5
Day Five: Being Your Mom 6
Day Six: Awake as the Spring 7
Day Seven: The Most the World Could Hold 8
Day Eight: Scream and Play 9
Day Nine: It Is Everything 10
Day Ten: Let It Live 11
Day Eleven: Learn How to Breathe 12
Day Twelve: On the Occasion of and in Anticipation
of My Daughter's First Heartbreak 14
Day Thirteen: Find the Me That Lives 16
Day Fourteen: Surface and Float 17
Day Fifteen: Love with You 18
Day Sixteen: My Own 19
Day Seventeen: My Own Rock 20
Day Eighteen: Safe Place 22
Day Nineteen: I Am Mine 24
Day Twenty: The Road More Traveled By 25
Day Twenty-One: Reflecting Rainbows 27

Day Twenty-Two: Beautiful to Me 29
Day Twenty-Three: The Tree.. 30
Day Twenty-Four: Beautiful Either Way................................... 31
Day Twenty-Five: Paint 32
Day Twenty-Six: Pieces of Truth 34
Day Twenty-Seven: Yours and Mine 35
Day Twenty-Eight: She Is on the Stair 36
Day Twenty-Nine: The Spice Is Wild.. 38
Day Thirty: Build It Beautiful 40
Day Thirty-One: Peace Crashing 41
Afterword.. 42
About the Author 43

Preface

You
Do not like a poem
Just can't seem
To see the point
And I must admit
That I feel sad for you
With all of your fingers
And toes
That when you have nowhere exactly to go
You can't simply live
In the words
And feel alive in the letters
Can't even seem to think in your mind
What might be the virtue in a rhythm and a rhyme
Without finding a task
Or a societal mask.
Though my thoughts are alive
And vibrantly on show
I could simply sit here and cuddle up with a poem
All day
I love them so.

Day One: The Ramblewood

The trees talk to me here
In this place
Don't they though,
Oh, don't they?
Down by the broken oak
That fell down and broke
Open
Such a long time ago
A laid down, hollowed out tree trunk
That thought its last thunk and lay to rest
Down where the whip-poor-will trills
And the robin calls his lady
And the woodpecker interrupts and knocks a hole
In the sound
That opens up the ground
Down in this rambling place
That splashes clean air on my face.
And oh, the green of the leaves
Through the rain that trickles down
And I,
I am found
At the bottom
Of the earth
On this damp and humbled ground
Barefooted
In mossy grasses
Squishing my toes
In mud
With a slap and a suck and a thud
Prickled by the stabs of pine needles
Letting go and looking up
Just to be there.
And I find myself
Where I am

Rambling along
Growing, alive
And up
And out
Reaching
To meet them all
So very small,
Looking up
Just to be.

Day Two: Fade Up the Skylights

Good Morning,
I say to
My bare feet
As they
Sink into dewy green grass
The light of day is already glaring
Around the yard
Just off my front porch
The world is waking
Too fast
Birds sing softly
A hint of happy
They float more than fly
As the sky lights fade up
Pinks and greys meet blues and whites
I look out and raise my hands
The breeze swirls all around me
I can see it, I believe,
Even though I can only feel it
I know it is guaranteed
My neighborhood begins to stir
The invisibly known cools my legs
Goodbye summer
Hello fall
Thank you, Father God and Mother Nature,
For this blessing of a promised changing season
I wiggle my toes
To give my answer
They are damp beneath
And warm on top
Like hot cakes
I go inside to write a poem
The day has started me up
And so I shall begin it.

Day Three: What You Dream Your Life to Be

Peekaboo
I see you
Laughing,
Raspberries
On your belly
I will always see you,
Silly girl,
Ringing around
Cuddling close
I got your nose
You have my heart
No matter where you are
Somewhere out there
My moon is your moon
Your soul—
Priceless
Like starlight—
Golden
To behold.
My dreams are
What you dream
Your life
To be.

Day Four: What Is True

You drive me crazy.
But somehow, we two
Are the same.
Your language is not
The same as my language
And yet
And yet
You speak to me
And I know
How the world works
And what it means
And I feel
Complete
For goodness' sake
I know my name
As I see it in your mouth—
And it spells out courage
And whoever I want to be
Because you are always exactly you
And I am exactly me
And what we say out loud
To each other
Means everything
That is exactly
True.

Day Five: Being Your Mom

It was boring and lonely
And exciting and ridiculous
Being your mom
Every day
I waited so long
Held you so tight
Only to know
That this is all so
I can let you go
And I will
And we two will
Move along
To be entirely our own
People
You grew me up
To be me
As you grew
And I am
So proud
Of us
For who we two
Will be.

Day Six: Awake as the Spring

It's almost my birthday
But it's been so cold
I don't want to . . .
I'm not ready for
A party just yet
The frozen earth is starting to . . .
Is beginning to thaw
But I'm just not so sure that
I am.
And still
The daffodils are growing green
Out of the dirt
And through the leaves
And budding
I can just about see the yellow
As a surprise to me
In this not-yet
Springtime
Is it eternal?
Is it perennial?
Is it me?
I want the new
I dream of the warmth
But so much still feels
So cold
The birth of day
The dream
Of now
Is it time yet?
I fall asleep
And I'm dreaming
But then I sit up
Straight as an arrow
Awake as the spring
And know
It's time to bloom.

Day Seven: The Most the World Could Hold

I saw it all
Every single bit
Your journey through open waters
In the bathtub,
Draining as you shivered
In cold air and naked skin,
Waiting for the water to swirl out.
The first time you saw a tiny lizard
Swivel out from underneath the porch steps
And over your tiny fat toes
And you squealed
With glee
As it raced away for its life.
I saw the whole of you;
I could have been out traveling the world
But I saw you instead
And that was the same—
No, it was more
Seeing the all of you
Exhausting
Exquisite
The most the world could hold
For me.

Day Eight: Scream and Play

I know I'm supposed to stay calm
And quiet
And uncomplaining about staying in the same place
For decades
But I want to scream and play
And laugh and run
I want to kiss anew
And alive
And velvety soft
I want I want
More
And to climb
Out of stuck-ness
And I am so sick
Of being told
No
Don't you do that
You can't be what you aren't yet.
What bullshit
Of the spirit busters
It itches at my skin
And I just want to jump in
And swim away.

Day Nine: It Is Everything

Lesson to my younger self:
Love is never linear
It is rocks
And rivers
Paved roads
And muddy caverns
It is sleepy
And hollow
Before it is deep
And rooted
It is veins
That cut to blood
There are bandages
And healing
Both
Of you
And of me
At once
It is your greatest nightmare
Before your most precious treasure
That's what it is
All of it
Is Everything.

Day Ten: Let It Live

How do you tell a love story?
Well,
First you get yourself a fire-breathing dragon
Then you get yourself some shattered glass
And some big hunking tears
Pouring out your marathon of sobbing
You purge yourself until,
Well,
Until your love wrings out and dries
And sounds like a giant ding-dong bell
Of majestic fairy-tale rhymes
Beautiful, big, and bronze
Only, sometimes, it is quiet as a mouse
When it needs to be for someone else
The power of a sound and a weight that could crush you complete
As the dragon burns you to ash besides
Love—how do you tell it?
Well,
You battle it to the death if you truly want it to live.

Day Eleven: Learn How to Breathe

The mind breaks open
Finally
And violently
Until you force yourself to breathe at its pace
Hyperventilate
And then hold it
And take it in
And say
No
Not this way
Like this
And you fill your belly up with air
Then release a great big wind of a breath
The way it should be
Creating your own breezes
And you know it
And you realize your eyes have been closed
Too long
To the colors
So bright
Around you
Thank God and Goodness
I remember how to do this
Like a baby
Free as a child
Who doesn't need to be taught
How to kick its feet
Green as the earth
New as the world
Blue as the breeze
Easy
Silence in your mind
Away with the noise
As though still in your mother's womb

Kept separate from the sound
That chained you to things you'd rather
Not keep
And there the memory is found
Throw out the trash
Hold on to what is fragile and valuable
Clasped at your chest
And through it beats your heart
Your hands know what to do
With that which is malleable
And your eyes
Closed and seeing
What is most precious
Now
And all the colors—
Magic.

Day Twelve: On the Occasion of and in Anticipation of My Daughter's First Heartbreak

My girl,
It's not you
It's always been him
He was always going to choose
The pretty little thing
With the shallow vanity
That reflects him back to
Himself
He'll choose ten of her
To one deep you
Because your heart is too big
For him to see
Your thoughts too enormous
The equation of you
Too great for his brain
So he'll wait at her doorstep
While she gets her mascara on
Just right
Because he can understand that kind of effort
He understands
Valuing yourself by looks alone
That's his language—
Skin deep.
And you—
Your heart and mind are an ocean
Of needing meaning far beyond
Such surface things
So bow down and say thank you
To the universe
That he is just—gone
And you can stand up into yourself
Because you are free to go out
Into the world

And find all the big bright beautiful things
That fill and reflect a big bright beautiful
You.

Day Thirteen: Find the Me That Lives

If I could I would but I can't so I don't and therefore I won't and that should be understood by me and accepted by others and not for me to wonder what they think about what I achieve or don't, and so I will stop for today, but in a way that is good practice for my own acceptance of self and also for others and our own limitations within, and our need to begin, but first to sleep and find our zest in all the waking rest until we remember that we can remind ourselves over to start to begin again— tomorrow, to brave all the sorrow and start anew and bid ado and say hello and make ourselves bellow into the vast great wide open mountainside, and say, *Why, hi there—I see you, new world, as I see myself, and I am here to find the me that lives in you,*
Today.

Day Fourteen: Surface and Float

It is the nakedness of self
Where your eyes light up
Looking into another's,
Fall knowingly and deep
The opal roundness of a cheek
On a heartbeat
In a dream
Though you be but wide awake
For it is the dream of true self
Reality that has become so sweet
That your lips taste the sea
And your face feels the salt
Sticky tangles of your hair
Across your face
And twists of brown silk masses
So lovely and splayed out
Behind you it dances
And you breathe
In the knowing that is now
Being fully naked in your life
Cool fingertips lightly touch the incoming bubbles
Feet buried in the sand
Waves washing
Tiny crashes over toes
And you aren't afraid any longer
Of storms past
Or storms to come
Because you know how to surface;
You know how to float.

Day Fifteen: Love with You

I fell
    From green
Into   my heart
With
You.
I cried   the ground
Absorbed   the sound
Deeply pulled   in
My roots
I tore   them out
To be   dragged
Back in
Chained   to   the earth
Soiled with   your
Dust   left
Among the rocks
Sharp and salty
To my taste
Threw
   Them
      Up
         They
   Crashed
  Back
Down
To the ground
Where I
   Remained
Rooted in
Love
With
You.

Day Sixteen: My Own

It's like I've just been given birth to
And I look at myself in the mirror
Puffy and splotchy
Worn out from where I've been
I start to cry—
Where am I?
It's all too bright
I need to be swaddled
And held
Wrapped up and rocked
I need warmth
And darkness
Calm and quiet
The cooing is too loud
Even if it's over me
Especially if it's over me
I need my mother
And I realize
I am her
Now.
The torch has passed
Shut Up! I scream
Please! I beg up at the giant faces
Quiet!
And they do
And they are
They dim the lights
Warm up the room
The sounds become soothing
I rest my hands on my chest
In a soft bed
And the heartbeat I needed to hear
To find the calm
Is my own.

Day Seventeen: My Own Rock

I Am My Own Rock
And this now,
It feels like the weight of the world,
It feels like breaking through the heavy glass ceiling,
But the walls are caving in,
And there's no way to break through it,
Without getting cut by a thousand shards on my way up,
I can see light overhead,
But glass is shattering down as I climb,
And still, I keep moving,
Finally knowing the way to go,
And sure as shit my fingers bleed,
By God they pulse down, the warm trickles of blood,
And I gasp with every single drip,
Every grasp my hands make for the next ledge,
But at least I'm finally, fervently breathing,
I hold steady to my rock: solid, true,
Friend or foe, this rock is my new foundation,
It is the base of what is there for me now,
And yet it's me who's lifting me up,
I may not know exactly where I'm going,
But it's my feet that let me tiptoe to reach up higher,
To the next landing place,
With my scraped and stubborn, burning knees,
Not so final, perhaps, but I've built myself up to be here,
I reach the circle of light
And I climb through
Even though I don't know what's on the other side
Of the above
Even if I don't know what I'm doing,
Where I'm going,
I Am My Own Damn Bloody Rock.
Now.
Battled, beaten,

Bloodied, bruised,
I earned the hell out of this now,
And so,
This Now is Mine.

Day Eighteen: Safe Place

It's your safe place
Our home
Where I have to remember
Not to yell
When you are gleefully squealing
Through the house
When you paint watercolors
Across the kitchen floor
And get as much of your rainbow
On the linoleum
As you get on the white printer paper
You make cardboard box cutouts into forts
Use my new throw pillows as the floor
Under your stinky feet
Flattening and dirtying them up
And I must remember to breathe
And smile
Soft and steady
For you
Because this is your childhood
Here and now
Your home
Your safe place
Where I let you
Be happy
You never knew there was a 'let' about it
Shouldn't have had to
Even when it wrecks my insides
Just a little
My new throw pillows . . .
I breathe a sigh
Not of relief
I let myself be worn out
Just a little

So that you can build yourself up
Into the adventurous and beautiful you
That you are
And boy, is it worth it.

Day Nineteen: I Am Mine

When I am free to be myself,
My self comes out of hiding,
And remembers that it likes to play,
When I say no to working more than half my waking hours,
For someone else's gain,
And gain my self back awake again,
When I walk barefoot in my own front yard grasses,
And feel the dew and see the sky as I look up,
And I speak the words,
Here is where I am,
And here I am me,
And I am here now,
And this hour is mine,
And in it, I am free,
To better know myself,
To better be myself,
To pick up my childhood heart,
Again and again and again,
To let it skip a beat,
As I jump a rope,
And though I may fall down,
Here is where I leap up laughing,
And remember and see and know,
That this time is no one else's to have
But mine.

Day Twenty: The Road More Traveled By

You took the road more traveled by,
Even though you often wondered why,
You're sure you wanted so much more than all the rest,
Why'd you settle for so much less?
You'll see your time through friends, foes, indifference,
Throw your hands up, say I guess this is just how it is,
You'll name babies instead of companies,
Drive carpool, make family schedules priorities,
Clean house, do dishes, drive all the same old roads,
Shrug and say this is just how it goes,
Even though you can't help asking,
What's still out there? What'd I miss?
Make the dinner, give your husband a deep kiss,
Hold the baby, rock the toddler,
Know there's nothing more precious than exactly just this,
And there isn't.
And yet . . . and yet . . . you know
You took the road more traveled by,
And no one, any longer, wonders why,
You knew that you were different than this,
But that this is what you'd truly miss,
Because everyone is different:
Families, friends, foes, fiends, fables, foibles, falls, fails, fortunes, finds,
Doesn't everyone kind of wish and mind?
This feeling of:
We made it lies in every story,
This knowing of truth, its gritty glory,
And the world will whisper,
There's still more out there for you,
But it lingers not so very far away,
It's with you, in you, all around you,
It's how strongly you decide that you can seek and find you,
And nobody else can see or do that for you,

No matter how much they truly love you,
You are you,
So keep dreaming digging feeding reeling being fighting lighting holding wanting fearing allowing growing knowing—and know:
That you built this
And keep building
Your little house of loves,
And what you love into being
Will grow.
It may be the road more traveled by,
But it's yours.

Day Twenty-One: Reflecting Rainbows

Rip the Band-Aid,
Embrace the cut knee,
Take delight in the healing that follows pain,
Cut the ties of fear,
You might never get there,
That desired somewhere place,
The horizon yet to be glimpsed,
And yet you already know you know it well,
Deep inside of you,
Already be-stilling your heart,
The dream
Of a daring child,
With dirty bare feet,
On the grass,
In between a small yellow house
And an old round well,
Deep and deeper and deeper still inside,
A place that bubbles up
Into a cup of water,
Reflecting rainbows off the wall
And the vision of a reflection
That your eyes make into a memory,
Ever so silly and ever so still,
Whimsical; only a child,
And yet a child knowing
What an adult
Can only barely hold on to as their own,
A piece of life only a child remembers,
In a whisper,
Remember . . . remember . . . remember
Can't you only remember
What that felt like?
And dance,
Hands twirling above your head

With abandon, like no other place,
And skip,
Crossing a field of tall grass,
To grandparents, arms outstretched and laughing,
To bees buzzing,
To grasshoppers hopping across the way,
And know the gentleness that surrounds you,
The soft nature that grounds you,
The breeze upon your face,
The rhythm of this place,
Always always always
There,
In your being,
Your beginning,
Unearthing the free reality of feeling:
A child of the whole.

Day Twenty-Two: Beautiful to Me

Sometimes for a minute
I'll think I look pretty
Not worn out
Or scraggly
Misshapen
Or haggard
But lovely
In my randomness
And so rosy cheeked
And tangled of hair
Just roused from sleep
Afresh and anew
Not embarrassing
Or ugly
As I drop my kids to school
Windows down
Waving
Wide smile
There's a moment when
No shame of being just exactly me
Is there
Just for a minute
Morning radio carrying me home
I'll start my day
Knowing I am beautiful.

Day Twenty-Three: The Tree

The Tree
That drips thoughts off its leaves
Like a hope
That you try to sustain
As you turn your face
Upward
Dangling free from a swing
Looking through branches
Grasping at bark
The arc of your life
From a childhood of longing
A time well lived
To adulthood
As you stumble up
Grab with your fingers
And all of your might
To climb higher
Swaying as the tree sways
To better find yourself
To better be yourself
To keep moving upward
As the rain trickles down
And now you know
Without a mouth turned down
That the way to move is forward
The way to go is up
And on every branch
There's an adventure to be found
Even when your feet slip
Even when your hair tangles
Even when your eyes burn
The sunlight is best seen
From the tippity top
Of the Tree.

Day Twenty-Four: Beautiful Either Way

Look
I will show you
Just what I mean to you
I don't have to
I'm just as good
Out where everyone else can see
There's nothing I need to prove
About a me to a you
But you're beautiful to me
And so I might as well
Show you
That I know my own worth
So you can stay
Or you can go
But I am wonderful you see
And in your reflection
I could grow
And so
The choice is yours
To leave or to stay
I see you are beautiful
But I'll be beautiful
Either way.

Day Twenty-Five: Paint

It's Okay
It's okay to feel lost
And still know exactly who you are,
It's okay that you haven't given yourself the time to be yourself for a while,
Because that's when you realize that you need to,
It's okay to want to toss your child out the first-floor window, two feet down onto very soft grass,
When he's being really really REALLY annoying,
And know that you would never do such a thing, and you will still kiss him good night,
And read him a bedtime story,
Because you love him fiercely,
And you'll make sure that he knows that,
It's okay to be bitter at the world when you realize that you used to really love to paint so much,
And haven't painted in ten years, and you ask why?
Why, world, did you keep painting from me?
When I loved it so?
Why did I let you do that to me?
It really is okay,
So long as you take back an invisible time in your day and you just go
And you paint and you paint and paint and paint
Some more,
And breathe a good God sigh of release,
It's okay that you hate ten percent—okay maybe that's an exaggeration,
Maybe it's one percent, but really sometimes also ten percent—of the things that your partner says or does or doesn't do or doesn't say,
Because remaining humble is knowing that he hates ten—no one, but also ten—percent of the things you say or do or don't say or don't do too,

And you both sometimes need to look at that,
And it will always be hard to look at,
But only after looking, and speaking, and knowing can you laugh
and see and know better all the things you love and need
And truthfully say, *wow, this person,*
There is no one I'd rather clean kid puke and pet pee off the kitchen
floor at one a.m. with than this person.
And you can also look at that person as you both vie for space
at the kitchen sink to wash your hands and know that you don't
know what you'd do without this "only bugs me ten, okay, fifteen
percent of the time" person.
It's okay if you feel lost and disconnected and lonely and what the
hell am I doing with my life? Some of the time,
For a minute or a day or a month or six but, hopefully only a day,
So long as you come back to yourself and look in and move along
and keep going and know,
This is my team,
I painted this canvas and then painted over it,
Every brush stroke was me,
I can paint me back into the movement,
Always,
Because I am me,
And it's okay.

Day Twenty-Six: Pieces of Truth

Take up your anger
And put it down
Set it aside and wish it calm
Maybe they deserve it
Maybe they'll never see why
Maybe you built it bigger
And made it the logic that was only yours
Maybe it's ten years old
And you exploded it like it was yesterday
Maybe that was valid
Because ten years ago
You knew you better stay quiet
Or else
This
Would have happened then
So there
You say
Now it's happened
Splat
Broken vase of water
On the floor
Ruining an oriental rug
Because it was always going to happen
And you can put it down
And choose what to pick up pleasantly instead—
The people who don't tell you to hush
Just because you reflect their shame
And the others—
They didn't know that when they told you *please don't say that*
That they were handing their shame to you.
It was always going to happen
So let the glass shatter
Leave it all over the ground
And there will now be tiny, beautiful pieces of truth
Broken everywhere.

Day Twenty-Seven: Yours and Mine

I had a life
Or did it have me?
I'm not quite sure
I was only twenty-three
With a marriage and babies
Holding the reigns
I loved it all so
It's hard to complain
About what was out there
In the world
That I may have certainly missed
I was yours
And you were mine
And what we lost
We never truly missed.

Day Twenty-Eight: She Is on the Stair

She
Is on the stair
And I
Hardly see her there
Separate from myself
As she stands unaware
For she is me.
And I am her.
And she is there
Just floating
She is who I was,
I am
Who she will be.
Could I ever be so proud
Of myself as I am
Of her?
Surely
Maybe
Somehow
But certainly
She makes me a better me.
She makes herself
Completely herself
For no one else.
As she lifts her head up
Smiles with satisfaction
Bright eyes
Crooked tooth
Round nose
Grinning cheeks
Perfection.
The flowing dress of a girl
Draped over the body
Of a woman

Becoming
Wiser than the insecurities
She'll be told she must hold
As truth
Braver than the voices
She'll be taunted to follow
Who dares tell her she's not enough?
I know her well
Because that's exactly when
She will stand up
And she will be the enough
Simply standing on that stair
Smart, strong, determined, divine.
She's all mine
To let go of
And out
Into the world
Where she reminds them
Just how bright
All the colors are.

Day Twenty-Nine: The Spice Is Wild

The spice is wild
This visceral child
He feeds me up
Until I am fed
Off to bed
Off with your head
You sleepy, exhausting,
Stinky,
Fiend
My greatest friend
Eyes that greet mine
With a grin
Every single morning
Though mine are barely open
His heart is holding
Me
How did I ever not know this soul?
His feet steady scampering
Through my life
Around my world
The kitchen island
He is with me everywhere I go
How did I ever think it so?
That boys would be so hard
And they are.
And there is so much to behold
So much he needs to know
About how to treat a woman
How that will say everything about
Who he is
And how that starts with
What his mother says
About other women
Ridiculous we humans are

But this boy
I love him so
And what I wish for him
Is that he be a good man
But for today
He shall cuddle up
On my lap
With sour cream and onion chip breath
And slightly sticky fingers on my arms
And I will sit in this perfection.

Day Thirty: Build It Beautiful

Build it Beautiful
Build it Bright
So that the whole universe
Is in your Basement
Twinkle lights plugged in
Children roller-skating
A dance party of make believe
Music fills
The room
Eyes closed
Voices echo
Soaring
Slinging into walls
Purple fairy wings
Scraped knees
Spinning around
And doing it
All all over again
And we all dance
And we all fall
But we get back up
And grasp arms
And look up at the stars
Twinkle lights on a Basement ceiling
And we swing
And we laugh
Because laughter in unison
Is our favorite thing
As we collide together
On the cool grey ground
All looking up
At our blanket of stars.

Day Thirty-One: Peace Crashing

I wish you peace that overshadows the weight
Of the day you are wading through,
I wish this peace to consume the warmth,
That spreads out into the water as you tread,
I wish you the peace of a maker of great things,
Of great deeds,
Of great humans,
The deliverer of babies,
And art,
And words,
And wisdom,
Who doesn't quite understand how,
But all the same was blessed to be the vessel of.
I wish you the peace of many crashing waves,
Subsiding back into a floating sea,
Perhaps not needing to question:
Where did I come from?
Maybe never needing to know:
How am I here?
I wish you waves crashing out loud the sound of:
Peace. Peace. Peace.
Peace to you, My Love.
My Self.
Crashing.
And
Out Loud.

Afterword

As for me
I will still
Believe in love
In all its intricately linked forms
Every single day
Like icicles on a Christmas tree
Shining bright
Even when dimly lit
And hopelessly melancholy
No matter what you
Believe in
And that to me
Is the epitome of a poem.

About the Author

Courtney Jett Walker spent half of her childhood on the Blue Ridge Parkway and the other half in the historic town of Orange, Virginia. It was a childhood filled with family, nature, and all things quintessential eighties. These places and experiences informed in her a deep sense of family and surroundings, community and aloneness, and attention to detail. Her love of poetry developed at a young age when she learned, almost as soon as she could write, that nothing describes what you see and feel quite like a poem. Now raising four children of her own in small-town Virginia, she wishes to instill in them the freedom to experience the world both together and alone, as a way of holding on and letting go of what it is to be human. Courtney lives in Scottsville, Virginia, with her husband, 4 children, 2 dogs, 1 cat, 6 chickens, 2 goats, and 1 beloved blue betta fish.

www.ingramcontent.com/pod-product-compliance
Lightning Source LLC
LaVergne TN
LVHW041346080426
835512LV00006B/650